Giant Dinosaurs

The giant plant-eating dinosaur
Apatosaurus.

Giant Dinosaurs

Text by
Peter Dodson
and
Peter Lerangis

Illustrations by
Alex Nino

A Byron Preiss Book

SCHOLASTIC INC.

New York   Toronto   London   Auckland   Sydney

ISBN 0-590-40275-7

Peter Dodson was involved in preparing the text but not the illustrations for *Giant Dinosaurs*.
Front cover painting. *Brontosaurus* © Douglas Henderson
Cover and book design by Elizabeth Wen

12 11 10 9 8 7 6   5 6 7/9

Printed in the U.S.A.   40

First Scholastic printing, May 1990

Contents

The Dinosaur Years   1

The Giants   28

The Discovery of the Giants   47

Other Amazing Discoveries   55

Pronunciation Guide   67

Chapter 1

THE DINOSAUR YEARS

How old is the oldest person you know? Sixty? Seventy? That's pretty old compared to you. It's hard to picture what the world was like sixty or seventy years ago. And the farther back you go, the harder it becomes. Try to imagine the world without cars or TV 100 years ago, or America with no buildings 400 years before that.

But how about going back 225 *million* years? That's when the dinosaurs first started to appear on the earth. The earth itself has been around much, much longer than the dinosaurs. It's four-and-a-half *billion* years old!

The dinosaurs ruled the earth for 160 million years. The dinosaur age is called the *Mesozoic Era*.

Many other types of life began to appear for the first time during this era. There were mammals, birds, turtles, frogs, salamanders, crocodiles, lizards, snakes, and flowers.

The Mesozoic Era was divided into three periods of time: the *Triassic* period, the *Jurassic* period, and the *Cretaceous* period. Different kinds of dinosaurs lived in each of these periods. In fact, most kinds of dinosaurs lived only six or seven million years before they were replaced by other kinds.

The first period, the Triassic, began about 248 million years ago. The whole world was cool and dry at the beginning of the Triassic period. For the first half of the period, there weren't any dinosaurs at all. But earth temperatures started to warm up. Then both dinosaurs and mammals began to appear. There were only a few big dinosaurs, like the 20-foot-long *Plateosaurus*. Most of the plant-eating dinosaurs and meat-eating dinosaurs were pretty small.

TIMELINE

Million years B.C.

	1.8 Quaternary	Age of man	present- 1.8 million years
	65 Tertiary	Hoofed animals and apes appear	1.8–65
	144 Cretaceous	First flowering plants Last dinosaurs	65–144
MESOZOIC ERA: AGE OF THE DINOSAURS	213 Jurassic	Middle dinosaurs	144–213
	248 Triassic	First dinosaurs First mammals	213–248
	286 Permian		248–286
	360 Carboniferous		286–360
	408 Devonian	First amphibians	360–408
	438 Silurian	First land plants	408–438
	505 Ordovician		438–505
	590 Cambrian		505–590
	4.6 billion Pre-Cambrian	Early life on earth	590 million–4.6 billion years

Remember: for prehistoric times, the higher the number, the farther back in time! For example, 200 million B.C. is longer ago than 65 million B.C.

The next period, the Jurassic, lasted about 69 million years, from 213 million to 144 million years ago. The earth was warm then. The earth's creatures grew larger in the warmer weather. This was the time of the great plant-eating *sauropods* and *Stegosaurus*. The 30-foot-long *Allosaurus* was the most famous meat-eater of this time. More animals appeared, too, including the earliest birds.

The *Cretaceous* was the last dinosaur period. It started 144 million years ago and ended 65 million years ago. During this period there were plant-eating dinosaurs called duckbills. Some duckbills had crests of bone and skin on their heads. These duckbills could blow through air tubes that were in their crests. They might have even made noises that sounded like trombones!

There were frightening dinosaurs with horns and spikes in the Cretaceous, too, such as *Triceratops* and *Ankylosaurus*. Near the end of the period came the ferocious *Tyrannosaurus rex*. There were also some small mammals we might recognize — like opossums.

Plateosaurus *feeding*. Plateosaurus *was a
large plant-eating dinosaur that lived in the
Late Triassic.*

The land was changing, too. For the first time, flowering plants began to grow on the earth.

What Happened to the Dinosaurs?

After 160 million years, the dinosaur age suddenly ended. About 65 million years ago, something happened that caused the dinosaurs to die.

Some scientists think a giant meteor hit the earth, causing a huge dust storm that blocked the sun's rays from hitting the earth. Lack of sun would have killed plant life, so the dinosaurs would have starved to death. Other scientists agree there was a dust storm, but they believe *volcanoes* caused it. There are many other theories: The dinosaurs froze to death; they died of thirst when inland seas turned into deserts; their eggs were eaten by mammals. . . .

No one knows for sure what really caused the dinosaurs to die. Scientists have been more successful finding out how dinosaurs *lived*.

Finding Out About the Dinosaurs

People learn about dinosaurs by studying their *fossils*. Fossils are remains left over from the distant past.

Scientists called *paleontologists* study and put together dinosaur bones. By doing this, they can find out what dinosaurs looked like and how they lived.

Imagine what it must feel like to dig into the ground and find a complete skeleton of a dinosaur, from head to toe. Most of the time, only bones or bone pieces are found. Sometimes a paleontologist will get lucky and find a huge skeleton, but usually it's missing a head, tail, or other part.

A lot happened from the time a dinosaur died until its skeleton was found by humans. Suppose a dinosaur died and sank to the bottom of a lake or river, or lay out on a plain that was flooded by water. There the body was covered by sand or mud (called *sediment*). Over the years, *deposition* occurred. That meant that the rain and wind brought more and more soil into the water. The skeleton was buried deeper and deeper. Over millions of years, the land sank beneath the sea. Minerals in the water hardened the sediment into rock and the bones into fossils.

But paleontologists don't find dinosaur fossils underwater. They find them on dry land! How can this be?

The answer is that much of the earth's land was underwater during the dinosaur age. In fact, a great sea covered the middle of the United States. But about the time the dinosaurs became extinct, the land began to rise, the water drained into the ocean, and the land became dry. Over millions *more* years, the land rose thousands of feet above sea level. And then wind and rain wore down the land, all the way down to the dinosaur skeleton. The bones began to stick up out of the ground.

And those are the bones the paleontologists look for.

Most dinosaurs didn't die near the water, so their bones were never preserved in the mud. Sometimes dinosaurs *did* die near the water — but their bones weren't preserved,

Earth During the Triassic

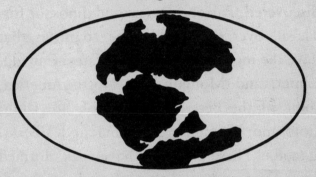

Earth During the Jurassic

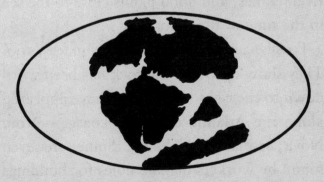

Earth During the Cretaceous

either. The bones might have turned to powder and blown away before they could be covered by mud. They might have been scattered or crushed by other dinosaurs. Even bones that come to the surface in the twentieth century can be destroyed by the wind and rain before a paleontologist finds them.

Still, many dinosaur remains have been discovered. Paleontologists find dinosaur fossils all over the world. The countries that have the most are the United States, Canada, China, and Mongolia. In North America, some of the best places to look are Utah; Colorado; Wyoming; Montana; and Alberta, Canada. These places all have rocks formed from sand and mud that were deposited in rivers, lakes, and flood plains close to the sea in the time of the dinosaurs.

Fossils can be found in other places, too. They show up where the rock has been worn down to the right level. Many have appeared along the Atlantic and Gulf coasts — from Nova Scotia to Alabama. Some are even found by workers digging holes for buildings or roads!

Learning from the Bones

Paleontologists are very careful when they discover bones. They first carve out an area of rock and dirt to expose each bone. They harden the bone with a special glue. Then they wrap the whole thing in plaster and burlap, and lift it out of the ground. One by one, the bones are protected this way. Then they're packed into wooden crates and shipped to a museum.

In the museum, workers remove the plaster wrappings. They slowly chip away at the rock that covers the bones. One wrong move could ruin the bone. They often use fine needles, dental picks, and small brushes. The bones are cleaned, mended, and preserved. Finally they are ready to study.

Usually the first thing a paleontologist does is measure the bone. He or she must decide what kind of bone it is, and what kind of dinosaur it came from. To find out, the bone is drawn or photographed. Pictures of the bone are compared with dinosaur bones that have been discovered earlier. If no match is found, the paleontologist may have discovered a new type of dinosaur!

Sometimes it helps to compare the dinosaur's head, teeth, or legs to those of modern, living animals. For example, if the dinosaur teeth are shaped like a giraffe's, then the dinosaur probably ate plants, as a giraffe does. If the dinosaur's leg bones are similar to an elephant's, then the dinosaur may have walked the same way an elephant does.

To find how long a dinosaur was, paleontologists may have to piece together sections of different skeletons from the same kind of dinosaur. So the skeleton you see at a museum may be the head of one *Diplodocus*, the tail of another, and the body of a third!

How can paleontologists tell how much a dinosaur weighed? Sometimes they make a small scale model of the dinosaur. They weigh the model. Then they try to figure out how many models it would take to make a life-size dinosaur.

Fossils have taught us many things about dinosaurs. From the rock around the fossils, we can tell if they lived near rivers or lakes, in swamps or on dry flood plains. Many liked moist, warm places where there were lots of plants. But they could adapt to dry conditions, too.

From dinosaur footprints, we know that many dinosaurs traveled in herds, but others wandered alone or in small groups. Some moved slowly, but others could put on bursts of speed.

From fossilized skin, we can tell that dinosaurs' skin was dry and pebbly, but we don't know about its color. It may have been a dull green or brown. It may have had bright bands of color like a coral snake's.

Most paleontologists say that all dinosaurs fit into just two different groups. In each group, the dinosaurs have one thing in common — the shape of their hips. One group is called "lizard-hipped," or *saurischian*. The other is called "bird-hipped," or *ornithischian*.

Some lizard-hipped dinosaurs were meat-eating. They walked on two legs and had slender, sharp teeth for slicing flesh. Some meat-eaters, like *Tyrannosaurus*, were very

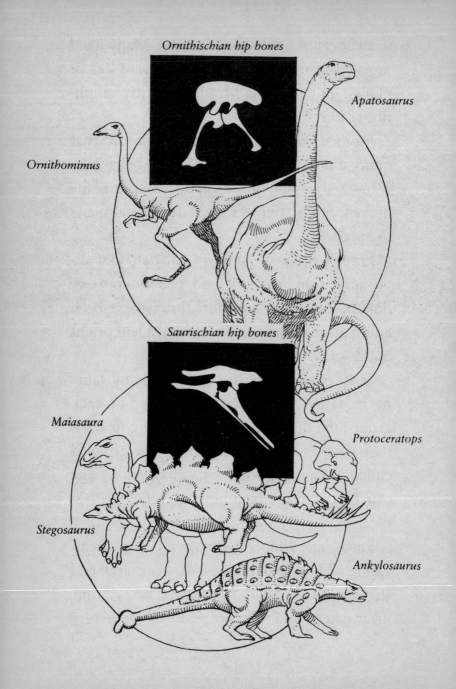

Ornithischian hip bones

Apatosaurus

Ornithomimus

Saurischian hip bones

Maiasaura

Protoceratops

Stegosaurus

Ankylosaurus

large. But many, such as the *Ornithomimus,* were much smaller. For example, the tiny *Compsognathus* was barely the size of a turkey.

Other lizard-hipped dinosaurs, called *sauropods,* ate plants only. They walked on four legs and had small heads. They also had long, snakelike necks and tails. Sometimes sauropods are called *brontosaurs.*

All bird-hipped dinosaurs were plant-eaters.

Some of these plant-eaters looked very frightening. *Stegosaurus* had sharp triangular plates along its back, and spikes at the end of its tail. *Ankylosaurus* was low and broad, and its body was covered with hard, armored plates.

Horned dinosaurs, such as *Triceratops,* looked something like rhinoceroses. They had huge heads with sharp horns near the eyes and nose. Out of the backs of their heads, bony frills stuck out to cover their necks.

How Big Were the Dinosaurs?

The word *dinosaur* means "terrible lizard." But dinosaurs were *not* lizards. In fact, most of them weren't even terrible.

More than 280 different kinds of dinosaurs have been discovered. And new kinds are being described every year. Some were as small as a cat. But the largest ones were larger than any land animal alive today. In fact, nothing even comes close in size to these giants.

Nowadays the bull elephant is one of the world's biggest animals. It weighs about as much as 80 fully grown men! That sounds pretty huge — but not compared to the biggest dinosaurs. They weighed up to 200,000 pounds. That's as much as 16 bull elephants, or 1,280 men!

Right: Dinosaurs compared to man. From bottom right: (1) Man; (2) Ornithomimus; *(3)* Psittacosaurus; *(4)* Compsognathus; *(5)* Coelurus; *(6)* Triceratops; *(7)* Camptosaurus; *(8)* Allosaurus; *(9)* Anklyosaurus; *(10)* Spinosaurus; *(11)* Stegosaurus; *(12)* Apatosaurus; *(13)* Lambeosaurus.

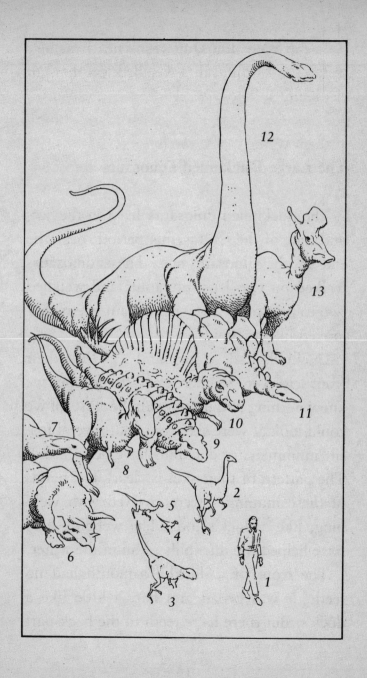

The average dinosaur wasn't nearly as big. In fact, most dinosaurs weighed less than an elephant.

The Large Duckbilled Dinosaurs

The duckbilled dinosaurs lived in the second half of the Cretaceous period, near the end of the dinosaur age. These dinosaurs walked on two legs, not four, and weighed two to four tons. They were plant-eaters that looked like duckbills.

Duckbills had strong hind legs, but their front legs were slender. For a long time, we knew nothing about their skin because all we could look at were skeletons. But several fossil "mummies" of duckbills have been found. The pattern of their skin is clear. The hands of these mummies were covered with webbing, like a duck's foot. The webbing may have helped the duckbills swim in the water.

The front of a duckbill's mouth had no teeth. It was broad and flat, a little like a duck's. But there *were* teeth in the back part of the jaw — from 700 to 1,600 of them! They were all tightly packed together. They ground up the toughest plants. And if any of the teeth wore out, new ones came right in to replace them.

Duckbills were strange-looking. Many had bony growths or crests on top of their heads. Others had hard, thin growths that stuck up like crowns. These crests and crowns were made of bone. There were narrow tubes of air inside. Perhaps they used these tubes to call each other. They could blow through them to make trumpet noises. When they got together, it might have sounded like a brass band!

But there may be another reason for the strange head growths. Paleontologists have found that the male duckbills had the largest crests. Maybe these crests were used to attract females — the same way a male peacock uses his tail!

Duckbills had large brains for dinosaurs. In fact, they had the largest brains of all the plant-eating dinosaurs. It's possible that duckbills were among the most intelligent dinosaurs, but probably not as intelligent as the meat-eaters.

Two examples are *Corythosaurus* and *Lambeosaurus*. They lived in Alberta, in western Canada. Their hips were eight feet seven inches from the ground. To wash the back of one of these dinosaurs, you would have had to stand on a step ladder. From head to tail, they were about as long as a school bus.

Edmontosaurus was a heavier sort of duckbill. It lived in Wyoming, Montana, and Alberta. Its tail was shorter than *Corythosaurus'* and *Lambeosaurus'*, and its limbs were longer and heavier. It weighed about four tons. That's a lot of weight to carry around on two hind legs. Its hips were almost as high off the ground as a basketball hoop.

Tyrannosaurus, the King of Them All

Duckbills and sauropods munched on leaves and grass. Even today the largest ani-

Duckbills Parasaurolophus *and* Corythosaurus *lived in Alberta, Canada, during the Late Cretaceous.*

mals on earth are plant-eaters — elephants, rhinoceroses, and hippopotamuses. But these animals have to watch out for meat-eaters like tigers and lions. Tigers and lions are smaller — but much more dangerous!

In the Cretaceous period, plant-eating dinosaurs had to watch out, too. They might run into the fiercest, most bloodthirsty giant of all — *Tyrannosaurus*.

Tyrannosaurus was a meat-eater, but it wasn't small. In fact, it was *larger* than most of the plant-eaters. The top of its *hips* was two feet higher than a basketball hoop — 12 feet altogether! When it stretched way up, it was taller than a small tree. But most of the time it leaned forward while it walked. Its head would be only a foot or two above its hips. That way it balanced itself and saved its strength.

Because of its tail, *Tyrannosaurus* was 40 feet long. How long is that? Picture a group of fully grown men standing next to each other, shoulder to shoulder. It would take about 24 of them to be as long as one *Tyrannosaurus*.

But the awesome thing about *Tyrannosaurus* was its skull. It was four feet five inches long. Compare that to your total height. Its teeth were six inches long, almost as long as your hand. The teeth were so thick that you couldn't close your thumb and your fingers around the bottom of one. But you wouldn't want to do that. The edges were serrated like steak knives. They could slice through flesh with ease. Such a powerful, fearsome skull has not been seen on earth before or since.

For such a large creature, *Tyrannosaurus* had little arms. They were strong, but only 28 inches long. That's only a bit longer than your arms! Their hands had only two fingers with claws. What did the huge *Tyrannosaurus* do with such small arms? Not much. Maybe all it did was push itself up from a squatting position. Or did it hang onto its prey and bite off a chunk?

But *Tyrannosaurus* didn't need powerful arms. Its feet had enormous, sharp claws. And it could lunge with its huge, heavy jaws. With those weapons, arms just weren't all that necessary!

The terrible Tyrannosaurus.

Tyrannosaurus lived between 68 and 65 million years ago — the same time as the horned dinosaur *Triceratops* and the duckbill *Edmontosaurus*. *Tyrannosaurus* probably attacked these animals for food. Some paleontologists think that *Tyrannosaurus* was too large to have run quickly. They think it couldn't have chased after its prey. They suggest it may have eaten only sick or dead dinosaurs. No one knows if this is true.

Tyrannosaurus lived just before the dinosaurs died out. Compared to other dinosaurs, it didn't last very long. Also, specimens of it are very rare. Perhaps there never were many tyrannosaurs around. Maybe they were too large to be able to kill enough food for themselves.

The tyrannosaur's full name is *Tyrannosaurus rex,* which means "king of the tyrant lizards." It's easy to imagine how it got that name. Its gleaming white teeth and red tongue must have been one of the most terrifying sights in the history of life on earth!

Other Giant Meat-Eaters

Tyrannosaurus was the last of the great meat-eaters. Before *Tyrannosaurus,* there were many other great meat-eaters. The deadly three-fingered *Allosaurus* lived during the Late Jurassic period.

A few million years before *Tyrannosaurus,* in the Cretaceous period, there lived the *Albertosaurus.* It looked a lot like *Tyrannosaurus,* only smaller.

Both *Albertosaurus* and *Allosaurus* were about 30 feet long. That's as long as 18 men shoulder to shoulder. Their skulls were about three feet long, the length of a yardstick.

Two allosaurs fighting. A ferocious meat-eater, Allosaurus *lived in Late Jurassic North America, Africa, Australia, and maybe Asia.*

Chapter 2

THE GIANTS

Sauropods — The Biggest of Them All

The true giants of the dinosaur age lived during the Jurassic and Cretaceous periods. They are called *sauropods*. A sauropod is easy to recognize. At one end, a tiny head peered out from the top of a long, long neck; at the other end, a huge tail. Its four heavy, straight legs must have shook the ground when it walked.

The sauropods were truly amazing dinosaurs. In fact, even the smallest ones were 40 feet long. That's larger than most other dinosaurs.

One of the giant sauropods, *Brachiosaurus*, was as tall as a four-story building. Another giant sauropod, 90-foot-long *Diplodocus*, was slender compared to other dinosaurs its size. *Apatosaurus* (also known as *Brontosaurus*) was much shorter than *Diplodocus*, but it weighed more than twice as much.

The tallest and heaviest of them is called *Ultrasaurus*. It was as tall as a five-story building. One of the longest dinosaurs ever discovered is called *Supersaurus*. It may have been 125 feet long. That's as long as four school buses.

What Were They Like?

These giant dinosaurs must have been rather slow. Their hearts and lungs must have been huge, to pump blood to all parts of the body and to provide enough oxygen.

The sauropods had simple, blunt teeth, because they were plant-eaters. With their long necks they could reach tender leaves at the tops of the trees.

We have a good idea of how the sauropods lived. Fossil footprints show that they often traveled together in herds. They would keep their young in the middle of the herd for protection from attacking meat-eaters. An adult sauropod was probably safe enough on its own — its size was enough to keep all but the most ferocious meat-eaters away.

Sauropods may have fed in swamps or lakes. But they probably spent much more time on dry land. There they could eat the leaves of trees. A herd of sauropods may have stayed in one place until they stripped all the leaves off the trees. Then they could move on to new areas with fresh leaves. They probably moved only one or two miles a day. Each year a herd of sauropods may have covered hundreds of miles.

Sauropods had very big bodies, but very small brains. A 10-ton *Diplodocus* had a brain only a little bigger than a cat's! A 40-ton *Brachiosaurus* had a brain the size of a large dog's.

Diplodocus *eating*.

Does this mean that sauropods were stupid? It would seem so. Sauropods had little brains compared to those of even the smallest meat-eating dinosaurs. Today's large mammals and birds have much larger brains than those of dinosaurs of similar sizes.

The greatest number of sauropods lived during the Jurassic period. Some existed later on in the Cretaceous period, but not as many. That's because a new breed of plant-eaters — the duckbilled dinosaurs — came along. Duckbills had larger heads, bigger brains, and better teeth for grinding plants. They took the place of the giant sauropods.

How did a 200,000-pound sauropod manage to get around? How could it have eaten enough to keep itself alive?

Paleontologists are still arguing about these questions.

Where Did They Live — Land or Water?

For a long time, many people believed that the giant sauropods lived in the water. When people first began discovering dinosaur bones, they didn't know what they were. It was the early 1800's. No one had ever heard of dinosaurs. Some people *did* figure out that the bones belonged to reptiles. But the only reptiles they knew about were lizards and crocodiles. So they thought th t dinosaurs must have lived in the water, like giant crocodiles.

In fact, one of the first names given to a sauropod was *Cetiosaurus*. That means "whale lizard." It was named in 1841 by Sir Richard Owen, a great British paleontologist. He thought the animal swam in the water like a whale.

Some people still picture the big sauropods in water. Artists often show them wading in lakes with mouths full of dripping plants.

Until recently even paleontologists thought sauropods lived in the water. They believed all that body weight would crush the sauropods' bones if they tried to live on land. Water seemed like a perfect place for them. After all, sauropods would feel lighter when they were in water — just as we do.

Cetiosaurus, *the "whale lizard."*

But careful study of sauropod bones has shown us a different picture.

Dinosaur bones are so strong that even 15 tons of pressure wouldn't crush a piece of bone the size of an ice cube. Fifteen tons is the weight of about 195 fully grown men! A sauropod's thighbone was thick enough to carry the sauropod. In fact, it was thick enough to carry *10* sauropods.

So the bones were more than strong enough to hold dinosaurs up on land. But does that mean they didn't live in water at all? Is it possible that they lived in water sometimes?

Fossils in Rock

Another way to find out if the sauropods could have lived in the water is to see if their skeletons are found or were buried near the water.

Paleontologists don't look only at fossils. They also look at the rock that the fossils were buried in. They study markings in the rock. Those markings show whether or not that rock was once underwater.

Were sauropod fossils found in rock that was once underwater, or rock that was far away from water?

The answer is — both! Sometimes sauropod remains are found in rocks that were laid down in lakes or rivers. But very often they are found in rocks that were laid on dry land. It seems that sauropods spent much time on solid land. They may have spent time in the water feeding on water plants, cooling themselves, bathing or even just crossing lakes or rivers to eat leaves on the other side.

Paleontologists had to answer another question: If the sauropods lived in water, how would they have been able to breathe?

Breathing Underwater

Water is very heavy. It presses against anything that's in it. The deeper the water, the greater the pressure. At very great depths, it can crush an animal's lungs!

Many sauropods had such long necks that there was a great distance between their lungs and their heads. If they went into the water up to their noses, they would die quickly. Their lungs could be as much as 50 feet deep!

So it seems unlikely that sauropods went deep into the water, although they probably waded.

Paleontologists also looked at the way sauropods were built. Did they have a body that was suitable for water living?

Many paleontologists compare sauropods to elephants. There are many physical similarities — heavy bodies; small feet; and four long, straight legs. Like elephants, sauropods had narrow, deep chests. And their small, round feet were better suited for hard ground, not mud.

Elephants do go into the water. In fact, they can swim across rivers. But they are primarily land-living animals as were the sauropods, according to many paleontologists.

What Did Sauropods Eat?

Sauropods ate only plants. What kinds of plants were around in those prehistoric times?

There were ferns and horsetails. There were plants called *cycads,* which can be found in the tropics today. Trees such as evergreens and gingkos also grew then and were probably a good source of food for the giant dinosaurs.

How Much Did They Eat?

To find out how much they ate, we can try comparing sauropods to large plant-eating animals of today.

Horses, cows, and elephants are all plant-eaters. They spend practically all day eating. A bull elephant in Africa may eat 375 pounds of fresh leaves and twigs every day.

Giant sauropods may have weighed 16 times more than a bull elephant. Does that mean they'd have to eat 16 times as much as an elephant eats? It would not have been pos-

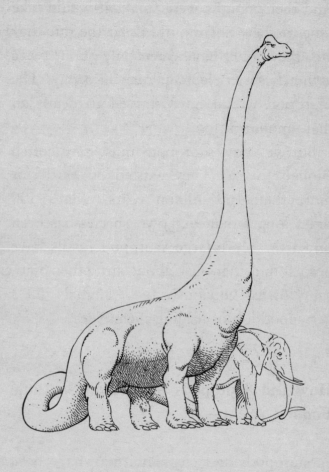

The sauropod Diplodocus *compared to the bull elephant.*

sible. A sauropod's teeth were not very wide. They could chop leaves but not grind them. And their mouths were small. It would take time to chew one mouthful. At the rate they ate, they could have eaten only about twice as much as an elephant does in a day. The sauropod would have starved to death on that amount of food.

But we know sauropods must have gotten enough to eat. They existed on earth for more than 100 million years. That's 500 times longer than our own species has been on earth. More large sauropod fossils have been found than just about any other dinosaur fossils. Obviously these animals did a very good job of feeding themselves.

How Did Sauropods Survive on So Little Food?

Sauropods and elephants may have been alike in some ways, but they may have been different in important ways. This might explain why giant sauropods could survive on less food compared to their size than elephants. Elephants (like humans) are mammals, and mammals need to eat every day or they will become thin and hungry.

But reptiles and amphibians, such as snakes, lizards, and frogs, don't eat as often. Some large snakes, like boa constrictors, have been known to live for six months between meals!

Why are these animals so different?

Mammals can stay alive only if their bodies remain at one constant temperature. For instance, the human body temperature must always be 98.6 degrees Fahrenheit. If it goes even one degree higher, a person has a fever.

The human body has to produce a lot of heat to keep its temperature at 98.6 degrees all the time. Heat is energy. Where does energy come from? Food! Our bodies "burn up" the food inside us to make heat and chemical energy. This happens even while we sleep. In fact, our bodies burn up so much food that we get hungry after only a few hours. We mammals are said to be *warm-blooded*.

The body temperatures of reptiles and amphibians get higher after they've been in the sun, and lower at night. If you have a pet lizard or snake, you know it's usually sluggish in the early morning. That's because it's cooled down and its body has lost its energy!

Reptiles and amphibians can live even though their bodies don't remain at one temperature. Their bodies don't have to keep making energy and heat for them. And *that* means they don't have to eat so much. They're called *cold-blooded* animals.

What about the dinosaurs? Were they warm-blooded or cold-blooded?

At first most paleontologists thought dinosaurs were cold-blooded. Dinosaurs were reptiles, and we all know that reptiles are cold-blooded. After all, cold-blooded animals can live on much less food than warm-blooded animals can. That would make it a lot easier for a huge sauropod to get enough to eat.

But in recent years, some paleontologists have claimed that dinosaurs were really warm-blooded. They say the dinosaurs' bone structure was similar to that of modern

Tenontosaurus *lived in North America in the Early Cretaceous.*

warm-blooded animals. They say dinosaurs' legs were suited for fast movement — they pointed forward like mammals' legs, or birds' legs, not sideways like crocodiles' or lizards'. And the distance between fossilized dinosaur footprints was large, which means they moved fast. According to these paleontologists, dinosaurs couldn't have been sluggish, cold-blooded creatures.

Is the warm-blooded theory correct? If it is, then warm-blooded dinosaurs must have spent practically the whole day getting food.

Surely some of the small meat-eaters must have moved fast and hunted a lot. They had large brains, sharp claws, and speedy legs. Maybe *they* were warm-blooded.

But what about sauropods? If they could eat only twice as much as an elephant could, would that have been enough for them to survive? The answer is no if they were warm-blooded, but yes if they were cold-blooded.

It could be that some dinosaurs were warm-blooded and some were cold-blooded. It could be that all dinosaurs were somewhere in between. No one knows for sure.

Albertosaurus *fleeing from* Tyrannosaurus. *Both meat-eaters lived in North America during the Late Cretaceous.*

It's one of the biggest mysteries of the dino-saur age.

We now have a good picture of the giant sauropods. They walked slowly through fields and jungles. They traveled together, stopping from tree to tree. Sometimes they even went into the water. And they were very busy — they spent all day eating!

Chapter 3

THE DISCOVERY OF THE GIANTS

Just from studying fossils, we know what dinosaurs looked like, when they lived, and how they ate. But who were the people who found these fossils? And what is it like to come across skeletons of the largest creatures that ever lived?

In the early 1800's, no one imagined that there were ever any other animals on earth than those that existed right in their time. All that changed when a doctor named Gideon Mantell introduced some strange, enormous teeth to the world.

As legend has it, the first tooth was found

by chance. In 1822 Dr. Mantell went to visit the home of a patient in Sussex, England. His wife, Mary Ann, was with him. While Dr. Mantell was working, Mary Ann decided to take a walk in the countryside.

Along the way, she saw something shiny on a piece of rock beside the road. Looking closer she discovered some large teeth. She showed them to Dr. Mantell. They both thought the teeth must have belonged to a large, ancient reptile never before seen.

Finally by 1825 the Mantells' theory was accepted and the creature whose teeth they found was named *Iguanodon* (meaning "iguana tooth," because the tooth looked like an iguana tooth of giant size).

In 1841 paleontologist Richard Owen coined the name *dinosaur* — "terrible lizard." By 1841 the remains of seven different kinds of dinosaurs had been discovered and named. In 1854 a series of life-size models of dinosaurs was unveiled in Victorian London. For the first time, the dinosaurs came to life. Dinosaurs have been a great hit with the public ever since.

Paleontologists were searching for dinosaur bones all over the world. One of the biggest early finds was made in 1909 by a paleontologist named Earl Douglass. He searched for weeks and weeks in the rocks near Vernal, Utah, but found nothing.

Just as Douglass was about to give up, he came upon a string of nine bones in hard sandstone. He realized they were dinosaur vertebrae, or bones from the spine.

Douglass had discovered a great "bone bed" as long as a football field. In the years since, at least 5,000 bones have been uncovered near Vernal. Several full skeletons and 60 partial skeletons have been found. In fact, the area is now known as the Dinosaur National Monument.

What must it have been like to discover a giant dinosaur skeleton for the first time? One of the most exciting finds was the discovery of *Tyrannosaurus rex*.

Finding the Dinosaur King

By now everyone knows about *Tyrannosaurus rex*. Your parents knew about it when they were kids, and so did your grandparents. It was one of the great discoveries in the early days of the twentieth century.

But in 1898, no one had ever heard of the "tyrant lizard." That's the year a young fossil hunter named Barnum Brown went to his first dig in Wyoming, where his team found an area full of dinosaur bones. There were so many that a shepherd had used some of them to build himself a cabin! This area became known as "Bone Cabin Quarry."

By 1902 Brown was working in Montana. Here the fossil beds were of the latest Cretaceous period — the very end of the dinosaur age.

He set up camp on a hot July day. As he dug in the sandstone, trying to find fossils, he came across huge bones that had never been seen before. Unfortunately the sandstone was so hard that the bones were locked in. It took *over three years* to dig them out.

But when the work was done, Brown had found something that must have taken his breath away. It was a nearly complete skeleton of an enormous dinosaur that Brown called *Tyrannosaurus rex*.

In 1905 the discovery of *Tyrannosaurus* was announced to the world.

In his long career, Brown made many spectacular finds. He became one of the greatest fossil hunters of the twentieth century. He worked for the American Museum of Natural History in New York. Because of him, that museum has the greatest collection of dinosaur remains in the world.

Brachiosaurus — The Largest Skeleton in the World

Most great dinosaur finds are made in dry areas with few plants. Those are the areas where erosion occurs. Erosion wears down the land and exposes fossils.

Surprisingly the largest fossil excavation in history was made in a low African hill, covered with tropical plants.

In 1909 German scientists went to Africa. They decided to dig for bones at a place called Tendaguru, which is now in Tanzania. There were so many bones that they hired 500 local people to help them. Never before or since have so many people been hired for a single dinosaur dig.

The dig lasted until 1912, and it cost a fortune. But there were great rewards. Nearly 100 skeletons or parts of skeletons were found. There was a small stegosaur, *Kentrosaurus,* which had spikes up and down its back. There was also a two-legged plant-eater, *Dryosaurus.*

Three or four kinds of sauropods were found, too. The greatest of these was *Brachiosaurus.*

The German scientists weren't the first to find *Brachiosaurus.* But their find was the most famous. They found eight partial skeletons. They also found the single bones of almost two dozen others. They worked hard to put the bones together. Finally they made a complete *Brachiosaurus* skeleton. It's the largest mounted skeleton in existence, and it

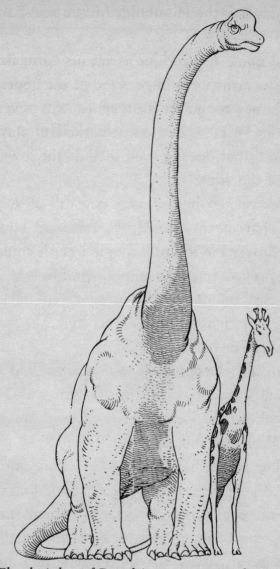

*The height of Brachiosaurus (39 feet)
compared to the height of a giraffe (17 feet).*

still stands at the Humboldt Museum in East Berlin.

The name *Brachiosaurus* means "arm lizard." Its arms were huge. One of the upper-arm bones found in Tendaguru was seven feet long — taller than most basketball players. And that doesn't even include the lower part of the arm!

The skeleton in Germany is a full 39 feet tall. That means *Brachiosaurus* could have looked over the top of a maple tree. It could have peeked into the upper windows of a four-story building. Even its ribs were huge. They were eight-and-a-half feet long, the size of a small bedroom!

Like all sauropods, *Brachiosaurus* had a long neck and tail. Its total length was 74 feet, about as long as two school buses parked one behind the other.

Other bones have been found that come from *Brachiosaurus* that were a little longer than the skeleton in Germany. Perhaps the biggest reached 43 feet high. Even so, the brachiosaurus was not the largest dinosaur that ever lived — but it comes close.

Chapter 4

OTHER AMAZING DISCOVERIES

Dinosaur Jim and His Giants

The world's longest dinosaurs were discovered by a man called "Dinosaur Jim." His real name is James Jensen. He's almost six foot six, so he may be the world's longest *paleontologist!*

Dinosaur Jim is one of the world's most successful fossil hunters. He found the first dinosaur eggs in the Western Hemisphere. And he's found so many skeletons that he doesn't even have time to dig them all up.

But his biggest find came in 1972. That

year Dinosaur Jim was searching for bones in the Dry Mesa plateau in Colorado. High up on the plateau, he came to a cliff. The cliff had red walls. There was a beautiful view of a deep canyon below. Right above that cliff, he found a bed of bones that belonged to dinosaurs that lived 150 million years ago.

Dinosaur Jim's team went to work digging. They found bones from all kinds of dinosaurs. But none of the bones were lying together in their natural positions. It was hard to be sure which bones belonged to which skeletons.

They kept digging. Soon they found the bones of a meat-eater no one had ever heard of before. That seemed pretty exciting. But it was nothing compared to a shoulder blade they found. It was so big they could hardly believe it.

Dinosaur Jim laid himself down next to the shoulder blade. He put his feet near one end. To touch the top of it, he had to reach all the way over his head. The bone was eight feet long. It was the longest dinosaur shoulder blade ever found. Dinosaur Jim and his team knew that other bones in this dinosaur would be even longer!

Unfortunately they found only one other major bone — a five-foot-long vertebra, or section of backbone.

Dinosaur Jim named his new dinosaur *Supersaurus* in 1985. To this day, only a little more of the creature has been found. But there's a lot that we can tell just from the shape of the shoulder blade. We can guess that *Supersaurus* was shaped like *Diplodocus*. It had a long tail like a whip. Judging from the size of the shoulder blade, *Supersaurus* must have been 125 feet long — maybe more! That would make it the longest dinosaur ever discovered.

But even with that discovery, Dinosaur Jim wasn't satisfied. When he returned to Dry Mesa in 1979, he found another shoulder blade that was nine feet long — bigger than the supersaur's! It also had a completely different shape. That meant it must have come from an animal totally unlike *Supersaurus*. In 1985 he named it *Ultrasaurus,* which means "ultimate lizard."

Supersaurus *eating*.

Dinosaur Jim kept digging for more *Ultrasaurus* bones. But just as before, only a few other pieces of the skeleton were found. So Dinosaur Jim carefully studied the shape of the giant shoulder blade. He realized it was similar to that of another sauropod — good old *Brachiosaurus*. Remember, *Brachiosaurus* used to be considered the largest dinosaur.

The brachiosaurus skeleton tells us what *Ultrasaurus* might look like. It would be shorter than *Supersaurus* — about 90 feet long. But it would stretch up more than five stories tall. That's much taller than *Supersaurus*. This massive creature would have weighed at least 100 tons, possibly 150. How much is that? As much as 20 or 30 bull elephants! One of its ribs would have been about 10 feet long.

Dinosaur Jim had a good way to describe *Ultrasaurus*. He said that if its stomach were a room and you were on the floor, you would have needed a ladder to change the light bulb in the ceiling!

But *Ultrasaurus* wasn't the biggest in everything. Like all sauropods, *Ultrasaurus* probably had a very small brain.

We don't really have much to show for *Supersaurus* and *Ultrasaurus*. We can only guess at what they must have looked like, and we could be wrong. Until we find more bones, they will remain mysterious.

In 1987 paleontologist David Gillette announced the discovery in New Mexico of a skeleton of a sauropod that resembles *Diplodocus* and *Supersaurus,* but it is apparently even larger still — perhaps even 135 feet long. The specimen is so large and the rock is so hard, that as of 1989 it is still being excavated. It has been nicknamed "Seismosaurus" because when it walked it would have triggered earthquake detectors called seismographs! Has the biggest dinosaur of all time been discovered yet? Probably not!

Mamenchisaurus

In the last decade or so, China has become one of the world's great dinosaur grounds. It has a center for dinosaur studies. New discoveries are made there all the time.

But in 1954, practically no one was digging for bones in China. No one — except a Chinese paleontologist named C.C. Young. Young was working alone near the town of Mamenchi. One day he discovered a strange-looking 71-foot-long sauropod. He called it *Mamenchisaurus*. It seemed to be related to *Diplodocus,* which had been found in the western part of the United States. Both dinosaurs lived about 150 million years ago, in the Jurassic age. At that time the land in China was probably very much like that in the United States. Both places had rivers, swamps, and flood plains.

Mamenchisaurus was an ordinary-size sauropod. It was smaller than *Diplodocus*. But its neck was 35 feet long, about half the length of its body!

The neck of *Mamenchisaurus* was a full six feet longer than the brachiosaur's. No one would have suspected such a long neck on a dinosaur its size.

What if the neck bones had been the *only*

bones found, with no other bones? A paleontologist would be tempted to say, "With a
neck this big, the dinosaur must be the largest ever found!" But of course, it isn't. This
teaches paleontologists an important lesson:
You can't always judge the size of a dinosaur
with just part of the evidence.

Shantungosaurus

In the 1960's, bones of a giant duckbilled
dinosaur were found in Baja California (a
province of Mexico) by a paleontologist
named Dr. William J. Morris. Before then
people thought that duckbills grew no longer
than about 31 feet. But these bones told another story. According to Dr. Morris, this
duckbill could have been 54 feet long. That's
almost twice as long as the longest duckbill
known! It might have weighed 23 tons, the
weight of over 300 grown men!

But paleontologists were careful not to
jump to conclusions, because not enough
bones were discovered. Maybe if someone

were to find a whole skeleton. . . .

They didn't have to wait long. A few years after Dr. Morris's discovery, Chinese paleontologists came across the shinbone of a huge duckbill in the Shantung province of China. They continued excavating in that area for four years, and found more than 30 tons of bones! There were bones that were even longer than the one Dr. Morris found.

A new type of duckbill giant had been discovered, and it was called *Shantungosaurus*. It had a low, flat skull.

A *Shantungosaurus* skeleton was put together from the bones. It is now on display in the Beijing Museum of Natural History. It's about 48 feet long, as long as four small cars.

Morris had said he'd found a giant duckbill. He said it was the size of a sauropod. The Chinese paleontologists proved he was right. *Shantungosaurus* was a spectacular dinosaur.

Shantungosaurus *lived in China during the*
Late Cretaceous.

The Search Goes On

For the last 150 years or so, paleontologists have often said, "I don't know." They've said it before each dig. And because they didn't know, they kept digging and studying. That's how they were able to find answers.

New dinosaurs are discovered each year. Every find helps us to understand about the prehistoric world. And one by one, those "I don't knows" have slowly turned into "I *do* knows."

Our knowledge of dinosaurs is still growing. Ten years from now, dinosaur books may include incredible creatures we haven't even dreamed of. By then we may also have answers to some of the old dinosaur mysteries. Who knows, maybe 10 years from now, some of you readers may make a discovery of your own!

One thing is certain: We will never know *all* there is to know about dinosaurs. But we will never stop searching. Right now there's something hidden from us under the ground — something that hasn't seen the light of day for millions of years; something new and exciting just waiting to be discovered.

Paleontologists aren't the only people who can collect fossils. You can, too. If you're interested, the best way to start is to visit your local museum. You may find there is a fossil club that makes trips to places where fossils can be found. There may also be helpful books at the museum.

Fossil hunters are at work every day, probably even as you read this. Each one of them hopes to find remains of a dinosaur that no one's ever seen before. Each year about six new kinds of dinosaurs are named. Many more will be found in the years to come. The more we discover, the better picture we have of life in the dinosaur age.

Pronunciation Guide

Albertosaurus	al-**bert**-oh-**saw**-rus
Allosaurus	**al**-o-**saw**-rus
Ankylosaurus	an-**ky**-low-**saw**-rus
Brachiosaurus	**brack**-ee-oh-**saw**-rus
Brontosaurus	**bront**-o-**saw**-rus
Compsognathus	**comp**-sog-**nay**-thus
Corythosaurus	ko-**rith**-oh-**saw**-rus
Diplodocus	dip-**lod**-oh-kus
Iguanodon	ig-**wa**-no-**don**
Lambeosaurus	**lam**-bee-oh-**saw**-rus
Mamenchisaurus	ma-**mench**-ih-**saw**-rus
Nodosaurus	**node**-oh-**saw**-rus
Plateosaurus	**plat**-ee-oh-**saw**-rus

Shantungosaurus	shan-**tung**-oh-**saw**-rus
Stegosaurus	**steg**-oh-**saw**-rus
Supersaurus	super-**saw**-rus
Triceratops	try-**serr**-a-tops
Tyrannosaurus	tie-**ran**-o-**saw**-rus
Ultrasaurus	**ull**-tra-**saw**-rus

ABOUT THE CONTRIBUTORS

PETER LERANGIS graduated from Harvard College with a degree in biochemistry. His more than 25 published works include *Time Machine #22: The Last of the Dinosaurs* and *Explorer #3: In Search of a Shark!*

PETER DODSON, Ph.D., is currently associate professor of animal biology and teacher of veterinary anatomy at the University of Pennsylvania School of Veterinary Medicine. Author of more than 30 scientific works, including *Evolution, Process and Product,* co-authored with his father, Edward O. Dodson, he has worked for a number of seasons in the dinosaur beds of western Canada and the United States. He is also co-editor of *The Dinosauria,* to be published in 1990 by the University of California Press.

ALEX NINO'S work has appeared in such publications as France's *Metal Hurlant* and America's *Starlog*. His paintings and illustrations have been published as portfolios, book jackets, and graphic stories. He is also the winner of the Inkpot Award.